Growth

From

Darkness

Book One – Stages of Trauma

Amanda Blackwood

Edited by Vicki Warner

MANDOLIN PUBLISHING

Published by the Mandolin Publishing Group
Amanda Blackwood, LLC
For more information, write to:
Amanda Blackwood
AuthorAmandaBlackwood@gmail.com
Or find us on Facebook
https://www.facebook.com/Mandolinpublishing
Copyright © Amanda Blackwood, 2023
Cover and internal design © Amanda Blackwood, 2023
Cover design layout © Amanda Blackwood, 2023
Edited by Vicki Warner of Vicki's Red Pen

This book and the teachings within are not meant to take the place of mental health applications such as therapy and medication that might be prescribed by a medical professional. The writing within is based on the author's personal experiences over a period of many years and is *not* the advice of a medical expert. Some names and characteristics of people mentioned have been changed, some events have been compressed. Randomly italicized words are for author emphasis <u>only</u>.

Chat with the Author!
www.facebook.com/AmandaBlackwoodSurvivor

Join the Talk
www.facebook.com/groups/growthfromdarkness/

THIS IS FOR THE TRAUMA SURVIVORS.

There are so many broken hearts in the world, but being broken doesn't mean good things can't come in the future. The journey may not be easy, but it's always worth the hard work.

Please take a moment to get a notebook to write in. Due to publication restrictions, space will not be provided to complete the questions in the workbook.

Growth

from

Darkness

Book One – Stages of Trauma

Chapter 1
Friedrich Nietzsche is Dead.

Are we our past?

People constantly tell us that "what doesn't kill you makes you stronger," but is that really true? Did the horrible things I've been through actually turn me into who I am today? Who does that say I am?

The quote above about 'what doesn't kill us' was originally an aphorism from Friedrich Nietzsche. He was a 19th century German philosopher. But being a famous (and long deceased) philosopher doesn't make him right. In fact, there are seven distinct and broadly accepted branches of philosophy, with thousands of philosophers per branch. Obviously not every philosopher can be right, and not all of them will have the same set of thinking. There are plenty of contradicting philosophers out there. And, philosopher or not, just because one famous smart person said something doesn't make it true. For example:

- Albert Einstein didn't believe black holes existed and said so on several occasions.
- Steve Jobs once said "I don't see most people using the web to get more information. We're already in [an] information overload. No matter how much information the web can dish out, most people get far more information than they can assimilate anyway." I'm glad he was wrong.
- In 2004 Stephen Hawking admitted he was wrong about black holes, and that some matter *could* escape them.
- Nostradamus made many predictions that did and *did not* come true, and has been called both a genius and a fraud in the same breath.
- Weather predictors are wrong on an almost daily basis. It could be snowing outside while the weather channel says there's no precipitation in the forecast for the whole week.

Sometimes people are just *wrong*. This includes famous (and not-so-famous) philosophers, but admitting that they could be wrong is actually a big part of being a *real* philosopher. Unfortunately, the ones who have passed away, like Nietzsche, no longer have the opportunity to profess such revelations. I did a little research into Friedrich Nietzsche in preparation for this chapter and discovered that the fellow had a few skeletons in his closet that he probably would have preferred not come out at any point in history, and yet we still attribute so much of our personal value and restoration to *one quote* he once said in the late 1800's. Perhaps we can reexamine the antiquated beliefs of the past and start to understand and examine the possibilities of our future now instead.

"What doesn't kill you makes you stronger" is generally an affirmation of resilience. On the surface that appears to be a great thing. Resilience is something to take pride in, is it not? But let's start to rethink this affirmation, consider what it's *really* saying to us, and come up with some of our own.

I'm no famous philosopher, and I've never taken a single class on philosophy, but I've come up with a few of my own philosophical affirmation quotes I'd like to share with you. I'd also like to invite you to make up some of your own on the next page. You don't have to share them with anyone or even tell anyone about them, but I'd like to encourage you to go back and read them once in a while, maybe add another when you think of it. Setting out some roots can help you to feel more grounded when you're going through the other exercises in this book. Feel free to circle or star any of mine you like, too.

- My experiences didn't make me stronger. I was already strong, I just needed to find that strength within myself.
- Peace within doesn't come from having everything we want, but from remembering who we really are inside.
- Someone's perception might be their reality, but it doesn't change who I am no matter what they think of me.
- I am not my past. I am a living hope for the future.
- Maybe I don't have it all together, but nobody

really does, so I'm in good company.

- I have nothing to prove to anyone but me.
- I am who I am, either because of or in spite of the people I've been surrounded by, but I won't be this person if I choose not to be.
- Every one of our body cells regenerate every seven years, meaning in seven years I'll be a completely different person than who I am today. And I'll like her just as much.

Now see if you can come up with a few sayings of your own that you think might help you in some of your lowest moments. If you're living in one of your lowest moments now, maybe move on to the next part and come back to this when you're feeling a tiny bit better.

Q: What would be a saying you can think of that would help you?

Who we are today is built on our memories, both conscious and subconscious. This is how the brain works. But it's also built on our experiences, as much as we would often wish that couldn't be so. So many of us have lived through truly horrible, horrendous things, and recovery has seemed so impossible for so long.

When I discovered that there was truly the proverbial light at the end of the tunnel, I often felt that it was far too distant for me to achieve in this lifetime. The fact that hope lay before me was too distant a concept for me to really feel ready to pursue it at all. Instead, I found myself struggling day in and day out just to keep my head above water and survive. People often told me that 'surviving isn't living' and I didn't understand what that meant. I was proud of myself for having survived everything I'd been through, but I had no idea that one of the things I found myself doing was called "trauma vomiting" in certain circles. I was telling some of the darkest parts of my past to anyone who would listen just because I'd finally found people who would listen to the darker details.

Many humans thrive on hearing the darkest details of humanity, but those weren't the right people for me to be talking to about the darkness. It helped me to talk about it, but I was traumatizing them with details they didn't need or want to know. I didn't understand that, and it didn't matter to me at the time. It was incredibly selfish of me to do this to other people, but I was so wounded I couldn't recognize it as being selfish. The only thing that my brain would process is that it was helping me to share the information because the more I talked about it, the less it hurt me. I didn't realize it was hurting so many other people.

I'm not talking about hurting the people who had injured me in the past by telling the truth of what happened to me. I didn't (and to some degree still don't) care about that aspect of telling the truth. It didn't occur to me that other people who were too polite to ask me to shut up were having to relive their own traumatic experiences because what I was telling them was digging up memories they weren't prepared to deal with yet themselves. I thought I was doing them a great service by showing them what it was like to have the 'strength' to talk about the past, when in reality I was causing them to have anxiety attacks and internal trauma that would cause sleepless nights in their near future.

It wasn't strength that caused me to talk about the details of having survived the trauma of human trafficking, but rather the obsessive need to feel like I was being heard by someone. I had few close friends and no family of my own. I *needed* someone to hear me and I was crying out in very unhealthy ways. When I think back on all the people I traumatized with details they didn't need to know, my heart breaks for them and I wish I could tell them how sorry I truly am.

I've found more productive ways to express who I am and what I've survived now in ways that leave people to understand that I'm open for healthy discussions, but that there are clear boundaries I will not cross and they're free to ask questions. These are things I'll address at the end of the book, but there are a few things we'll need to cover before we get there.

Chapter 2
Understanding the Connection

Is there a connection between

events and impacts?

It's never necessary to dig up every single experience we've ever had in our lives in order to move on with living, but understanding the connection between events and impacts is fairly important. These things are definitely a part of who we are, and they should be recognized as having formed what are called neural-synapses in our brains, meaning they literally rewired our brains to think in new ways. Think of it this way: new neural-synapses are new connections, new commands, and we need to understand those connections to understand how to move beyond them.

While it might seem perfectly normal to walk away from a pair of jeans we no longer fit into and that serve no purpose in our lives, it's much less common for us to walk away from ways of thinking that no longer serve a purpose in our lives. They have also lived to the end of their potential, but letting them go is almost as difficult as tossing out that ratty old sweat shirt we love, even though it's full of holes and doesn't keep us warm anymore. It's served its usefulness, and yet we can't just discard it. Some of our brain rewiring sticks with us much the same way, and that rewiring can affect our lives and relationships in some not-so-positive ways. These memories, synapses, and experiences can rob us of truly amazing lives.

There was a time I did this myself. I was living as though my past was also my present, and everything I'd ever see in the future. That's not the kind of life we were meant to live. Once I started to realize that, I experienced a massive shift in my thinking. But that massive shift had years of self-conditioning to fight against, and my way of thinking needed to be re-trained, forming new neural-synapses over time and exposure to this new way of thinking. The past doesn't exist just to limit our present and future, but that's exactly where so many of us find ourselves.

Take a moment to write down a shortlist on the next page of some things you have in the room with you now that could possibly be tossed away and never missed.

Q: What are some things you could throw out and not miss having?

If our past is constantly repeating, it might be because we are hanging on to those memories, or even things or people, who no longer serve a healthy purpose in our lives. We have to learn to let go of them.

Oh, what a painful lesson that was for me. I'd been working on a project for work when I opened up a desk drawer and found a small round lighter hidden all the way in the back of the drawer. I'd forgotten about it long ago. It was a lighter my former trafficker had given to me. Without understanding or explanation, I burst into tears and shoved that lighter back into the desk drawer 'for safe keeping' rather than throwing it in the trash where it belonged. I kept it for a number of years after that, too. I just avoided going back into that desk drawer for a long time. That avoidance was extremely unhealthy.

Now write down the things in the room that are connected to old memories that might not be the most pleasant, like that disposable lighter I found. You might not even see them, but we all have a few tucked away somewhere.

Q: What are some things in the room connected to unpleasant memories?

Think for a moment about throwing those things away. Close your eyes and imagine what your space would look like if those things weren't there. Would you replace them with new things? Would those things have new memories attached to them of a more pleasant nature? What would those things be, if you could go get them right now and money was no object. Would you purchase a mantle clock that keeps time with your heartbeat to remind yourself that you're still alive? What about a large painted portrait of a loved one? Perhaps you'd leave the space empty, waiting for you to return from a whirlwind trip to Paris or London with souvenir shop finds?

Q: What would you fill your space with?

It is my sincere hope that you may have used up more space to list the things out that you'd replace old things with. This is the start of forming those new neural-synapses I was talking about earlier. It's time to start thinking about a more positive future, even while still focusing on the trauma recovery process.

Some people believe that we must examine every detail of our past to make sense of it and move on from it, such as a therapist or counselor. Others believe that the past is the past and should remain - well, in the past. They don't want to talk about it, they don't want to think about it, the past has no influence on anything that might happen today. While both of these philosophies might work depending on the person, the wrong philosophy can cause irreparable damage to a person. What works for John might not work for Sue. That's true of all things, down to the shape and size of our undies. People need to find what works best for them, and nobody on the planet can tell them what that might be until they discover it for themselves. For me, talking about it helped me and hurt others. Therapy, once I discovered the damage I'd done to others, was my new outlet. Then came writing, painting, research, and discovery.

Eventually, the thing that helped me the most was learning why my brain worked the way it did, how things were connected to my reactions, and what I could personally do to fight against it in healthy, productive ways. So I wrote my autobiography, painted my memories, researched mental health, studied trauma recovery, and became an expert in my field. That exact path is unlikely to help everyone else on the planet, but I always try to encourage other people to try it.

Q: What have you tried so far to help aid in your own recovery?

Have you seen a therapist or counselor? Did you try journaling? Have you tried painting or drawing? Have you looked into art therapy? How many self-help books have you read? Have you found anything so far that seemed to help you more than anything else?

Q: What do you wish you could try next?

Do you have plans to try anything that's been suggested to you by someone you know? Have you been thinking about seeing a mental health professional, or taking a class?

Q: What do you plan to try?

This might be something worth circling in your notebook. Thinking about the things you plan to try should be a more central theme in your life. You're ready and looking for help, but the first steps are up to you.

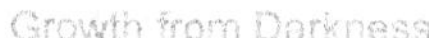

Growth
from
Darkness

Book One – Stages of Trauma

Chapter 3
Stages of Trauma

What are the stages of trauma?

When I'm interviewing guests for my trauma recovery podcast, one of the questions I always ask them is how their experiences have an effect on their lives even today. Every single one of my guests on the show have always admitted that the effect is there, and recognizable, even many, *many* years after the event. Sometimes the effect has a positive outcome, like the many survivors who are now therapists and counselors and focus their lives on helping others. Often it's a habit that's formed from repetition, such as looking over our shoulder in a parking lot, or walking with keys laced between our fingers. The results vary from one person to the next, just like the experiences do. While two people may have survived the same trauma classification, such as domestic violence, no two experiences are the same. The coping mechanisms and habits formed in the wake of trauma are never the same either.

The basic stages of trauma are very similar to the stages of grief. It makes total sense when you think about it. You're stuck in a place of grief without thinking about it. Even though you're not grieving for a loved one, in a way you still are. You're grieving for the person you once were, because your body and your brain already recognize that the person you were will never exist again. You've been permanently changed in ways you couldn't have predicted. While you might still be wishing to rekindle that innocence you once knew, the truth is that the innocence is now gone and in its place you have this memory you might wish would never exist. Those new synapses have been formed and your brain has been permanently rewired.

Trauma and grief both can result in a lot of similar emotions: grief, despair, withdrawal, loss, loneliness and more. The loss of a loved one can trigger trauma, too. Sometimes when that happens it's hard to understand what you're feeling, and if it's selfish to feel it at all. Traumatic events, no matter what they are, can stir up things within us that we don't exactly *want* to feel, but we simply don't have control over *what* we feel. We can, however, control how much our emotions control *us*.

Five Stages of Trauma

The five stages of trauma are not linear. They're outlined in the same order each time you ever see the list, but that doesn't mean you'll systematically filter from one to the next until you're complete with the process. In fact, this rarely ever happens, and if it does you should count yourself as extremely fortunate. Instead, it's perfectly normal to shift from one to the next and back again, multiple times. Sometimes it's possible to feel several of these emotions at the same time. Going through them in a matter of minutes is something only possible through the miracle of cinematic lenses. Ah, Hollywood Magic. If only life could work like that, with the pause button for good times, the rewind button for reliving favorite memories, and a fast forward button for speeding our way through recovery. Unfortunately we have to do the real work of powering through even the most painful of times if we want to move on to better things in our futures.

The five stages of trauma (and grief) are outlined as:

1. *Denial*
2. *Anger*
3. *Bargaining*
4. *Depression*
5. *Acceptance*

Each one is a world of its own; the cold, unrelenting emotions our brains force us to feel can be isolating, but there is hope. My purpose in writing this is to help you find it.

Q: Where do you think you are in the trauma recovery stages now?

Chapter 4
Stage 1: Denial

What is denial?

There are two different forms of trauma denial. This chapter will exclusively examine the survivor's denial. However, there is another form of trauma denial that should be addressed later on and will be included in the "Supporting Survivors" volume. (This other form of denial is sometimes referred to as the 'second wound' and occurs when the survivor is blamed for the abuse, or when friends and/or family try to deny the abuse ever occurred.)

When I first got away from my trafficker, I was proud of myself. I didn't recognize what I'd been through was anything beyond just having been in an 'abusive relationship' but my brain wouldn't allow me to process anything else. I tried to tell people, but I couldn't find the words. In so many ways, I didn't want to find the right words because I believed any scenario would paint me as being at fault, and I didn't think I could take that anymore. I was afraid if I said it out loud, I might start to blame myself for what happened, too.

It took me 8 years to learn that what I'd survived could even be classified as human trafficking, and by then I was finally ready to talk about it. Still, my brain released only portions of my memory to me at a time to prevent me from going into the information overload I quoted Steve Jobs on in chapter one. It was the only way my brain had to control the situation enough so I didn't end up a crumpled mess in a group recovery home I couldn't afford on my limited income. My brain understood that I couldn't afford mental health services, and so my brain did what it could to protect me.

Going through something traumatic can (and often does) change the way you perceive the world. It's amazing what trauma can do to us. Trauma can go so far as to take people out of our lives - friends or family we thought we would have with us forever. It can change our physical body in visible and invisible ways, from the loss of a limb to an autoimmune disease that leaves us internally struggling to survive from day to day. (If you've never read Christine Miserandino's "Spoon Theory" I highly recommend it.) Of course it all depends on the trauma that each of us experiences, and our internal coping mechanisms.

In 2015 a study was done that connected autoimmune issues with emotional abuse and trauma. That was four years after I'd escaped human trafficking, and only one year after I'd been diagnosed with Crohn's Disease, which is an autoimmune disorder. At the time of my diagnosis, nobody had any idea what might have caused it or what it might have been linked to. It wasn't believed to be hereditary, but nobody knew for sure. I went so far as to call my parents to ask if anyone else in the family had Crohn's Disease simply to find out. "Not that we are aware," I was told. (Immediately afterward my sibling told a mutual friend of ours that I had claimed to have cancer and asked my parents to sell everything they owned to pay for my cancer treatments. I look back at that now and laugh, but at the time it was infuriating and caused several trauma responses.)

Going through these physical and mental changes can sometimes be quite overwhelming and might delay our having to think about the traumatic event that caused the changes in the first place, especially if we don't know that the trauma was what caused the change to start with.

Denial is considered the first stage of trauma and grief because it's a type of defense mechanism. It helps to reduce the impact of what you've experienced so that you might have more time to evaluate what happened to you when you might be more ready to do so. The initial blow can be devastating, and our brains do what they can to protect us.

While denial is a protective measure, it won't last forever. As much as we want to ignore what happened to us, eventually we will need to face the new reality. That will lead us into facing the emotions, the PTSD, and the numerous trauma reactions associated with those emotions.

The protections our brains offer with denial can be helpful, of course. The automatic reaction has a purpose. It keeps us from having to confront frightening and confusing emotions, and helps to keep those traumatic memories away from our forethoughts. However, denial can also leave you feeling numb. You aren't free to feel your real feelings. You can't connect with other people. As much as we don't want to do it, we must move into a place of understanding that something happened to us. Our reality has changed. Our experience exists. Starting with something simple, list a few things in your notebook that you've struggled with accepting in the past. I'll go first.

1. My first marriage was not healthy but I stayed because I had nowhere to go.

2. Cookie (my childhood dog) disappeared during a flood and I wanted to believe she had escaped, and someone else took her in.

3. I've never been close to my family, even though I tried many times to have a

relationship with them.
I survived a terrible thing.

Now it's your turn. Don't push yourself too hard unless you're ready to get into the hard stuff.

Q: What have you struggled to accept in the past?

It's important to start to understand these things about yourself so that you can learn why you react the way you do to some seemingly unconnected things. It's amazing how often things are connected in our brains even when we try to tell ourselves that they're not. Please feel free to share your answers in the Growth from Darkness alumni Facebook group.

www.facebook.com/groups/growthfromdarkness/

Chapter 5
Stage 2: Anger

Anger is a stage of trauma?

This was a hard one for me. I'd worked so hard and pretended for so long that I wasn't angry at what had happened to me that it was a delicate lie. I felt like a bucket filled with water to the brim, and any little thing that added even one more drop of water would release a torrent of rage all over the offender. It caused so many issues in relationships that I constantly alienated people until I had no true friendships left in my life. The anger inside caused so much isolation that I resigned myself to just living alone for the rest of my life. "Maybe I'm better off that way," I thought. "People only end up hurting me anyway. This way I won't get hurt anymore." *Oh, how wrong I was.*

Moving past the denial of a traumatic event can take time, but once you're past that one, the rest of the world sort of opens up for you - and it's scarier than you might have imagined. The reality of what you survived starts smacking you upside the head like a brick being thrown from a fifth floor window. Being bombarded by that emotional overload starts to bring up all sorts of emotions you might not be ready for. The key emotion that will seem to take over everything is anger. Reality screams at you, and in turn, you want to scream right back.

Experiencing the emotions and memories related to the trauma that you've survived is much like reliving the experience again. You may have flashbacks and other symptoms you're not prepared for. Anger is absolutely a normal, natural response. You might feel anger at things you'll be surprised that you're angry about, too. You could be angry over the loss of a friendship or the passing of a loved one, or the loss of a former ability. With the loss of a limb, it might be impossible to type, or hug a friend, or run like you once did. With emotional trauma, it's perfectly normal to be angry about the injustice of what you experienced, or that the person who harmed you hasn't had to face any repercussions. Much of my own anger was recognizing that my former trafficker was still free to perform his duties as a police officer, even in spite of my reporting him to his superiors. Whatever the reason behind the anger, just know that it's a common and normal response to having survived trauma of all kinds.

Anger, like denial, is another coping mechanism. Feeling that level of anger allows you to feel something, *anything*, without having that be an overwhelming flood of sadness, grief, pain, etc. It helps to mask them so they don't take over completely. The "anger" stage of trauma can last longer than anything else sometimes, depending on the person and the experience. It can manifest in many ways you might not expect. Often people are shocked. One young woman came to me last September and told me that she didn't realize she was angry because of the way that her anger showed up. She'd turned sarcastic and bitter, wanting to isolate from people she loved. When she realized what her symptoms meant, she asked for help to manage and move on from them. She was the first person I was able to help with the program I'd developed through Growth from Darkness.

Some of the ways that anger can show up in your daily life that you might not be expecting are things that you might think you've just developed as a part of your personality. In a way that's correct, but these things might change once more when the internal anger has been recognized and managed. Take the time to circle all of the anger reactions below that you've experienced in the past month.

- *Irritability*
- *Anger outburst*
- *Defiance*
- *Anger at inanimate objects*
- *Isolation*
- *Opposition*
- *Sarcasm?*

Yep. *Sarcasm.* I had become a sarcastic, defiant, isolated, irritated *hothead.* I barely recognized myself.

No wonder I'd lost my most prized friendships. Even the most loyal of friends will take only so much before they find companionship elsewhere. But when that happened, I blamed *them* for not being there for me! Outbursts of a trauma survivor don't always have to be directed at people, and they don't always have to be just anger.

Sometimes my outbursts were directed at things like a salt and pepper shaker I'd had for years. I smashed the porcelain salt shaker against the wall one day in a horrible memory of abuse where salt had been a weapon against me. I'll avoid sharing any of the details, but the very presence of the salt shaker the morning of an awful nightmare flashback triggered an emotional reaction from the memory, and that salt shaker had to pay the ultimate price. The lighter, meanwhile, still remained in the back of the desk drawer. The 'triggers' might be surprising and often unpredictable.

One of the many useful ways to help you understand your anger is with a good therapist. Therapy can absolutely work wonders, but many people (myself included) are uncomfortable with the very idea of talking to a therapist.

One of my early clients told me that she didn't want to seek therapy because she felt that her story was her own and she shouldn't be forced to tell it to anyone. Many people feel that way. But that meant she had to do the work on her own without the guidance of a therapist or counselor to figure out what was causing the anger, and what other emotions it might have been covering up. This same client, we'll call her Susan, worked with me for quite some time. She eventually discovered that her anger was having some pretty awful impacts on not just her personal relationships, but her professional relationships, too. She had been working as a lawyer in the same firm for fifteen years, and over the last two years after a traumatic event, she'd isolated herself from everyone at work so much that the firm was debating on whether or not to ask her to leave the office permanently.

Her anger had gotten completely out of hand. She recognized that she did need some professional help. While she still staunchly refused to see a therapist or counselor, she did enroll herself in some anger management classes that helped her to find new and more productive ways to cope. She had a meeting with her colleagues at the law firm and let them know what had been going on. They're now working on a full reconciliation. That anger management class never required that she share her personal story of trauma with anyone, but helped her find better ways to manage her emotions.

Think about the last few times you were angry and did or didn't understand why. Take a few minutes to write about the experiences. Did you learn anything from them? Do you know why you were so angry? Who or what were you angry at? What was that experience like? Did you experience any of the bullet points?

- *Irritability*
- *Anger outburst*
- *Defiance*
- *Anger at inanimate objects*
- *Isolation*
- *Opposition*

- *Sarcasm*

Try to be as thorough as possible when you answer this question in your notebook. Remember, you don't have to share it with anyone. Keep your answers handy, you'll be referencing this exercise again in the future.

Q: When was the last time you were angry and didn't understand why? Which of the bullet points do you remember feeling at that moment? Refer back to the bullet points on the previous page for reference when you're answering this question in your notebook.

Chapter 6
Stage 3:
Bargaining

How do I make it stop?

"Maybe things will be different if I just start over somewhere else."

"What if I had never gone there?"

"God, please take this pain away, I'll do anything."

I personally said every one of those phrases in my first years of freedom. I even lived the first one when, in 2016, I loaded my cats into a rental truck and drove

1,000 miles away from my home of 14 years in search of a new start in Colorado. For many survivors of trauma, the above phrases are all too familiar and can bring tears to our eyes.

After we somehow manage to work through denial and learn to start coping with the anger, all of the underlying emotions connected to the trauma we survived start to become much more clear. It can be so overwhelming that the intensity is often too much and we don't know how to cope with it all. You're finally getting a first look at the real magnitude of what you've lost or what you've been through. At this point it's an overwhelmingly natural response to want to gain control of your situation. The only way the brain can conceive of to get that control is through bargaining, though often through irrational means. (I feel it's important to include that some people never find themselves in the bargaining stage of trauma, but that is extremely rare.)

There are a few different ways that bargaining can show up in your life, and not all of them in ways you might be familiar with. A person might wish that things were different than they currently are. They might pray for the trauma to have never happened. The mind can delve into the 'what if' scenarios that include different outcomes than the foregone conclusion. Every one of them is painful, and it can be so easy to get lost in the bargaining stage. It's one of the coping mechanisms we have that is designed to postpone reality. But the past can't be changed (unless we find the magic time machine) and we have to move forward with our lives, as uncomfortable as that is.

Q: What was at least one bargaining scenario you can remember using after a traumatic event in your past? Writing it down will help you solidify what I'm talking about.

It can be really easy to distract yourself from reality using the bargaining tool your brain conceives, it won't help you to face things and help you to move on. Think for a moment about what bargaining and what-if scenarios can change, if anything. The best way to move beyond this stage is by challenging those thoughts. All they're doing is distracting you.

Q: What, if anything, can any of your process of bargaining change for you?

Bargaining is our brain's way of tricking us into thinking we can control the situation. That desire for control is a trauma response I'll be covering in book two.

Chapter 7
Stage 4:
Depression

Should I just get over it?

It's been a roller coaster. Your emotions have been all over the map and you've struggled to focus on what 'real life' might look like after having experienced the trauma you've survived. You've been distracted and focused on everything under the sun *except* what you've needed to focus on. Now, emotions are starting to even out, and the quiet stage of depression moves in like an unwelcome roommate.

This was a terrible place for me. I'd always been such an optimistic person, and suddenly I was quiet, reserved, sad, lonely, and a myriad of other things that could only be described as 'depressed' but I wasn't ready to admit that it was depression. I was bouncing back to the denial stage of things. I simply couldn't face that my personality had been changed forever because of what someone else had done to me. It was devastating. It was also 2020 in the midst of the pandemic when this stage hit me, and the whole world was depressed right then. But there was good news just over the horizon.

The depression stage is nearly the end of the process of coping with trauma. It wouldn't be long before I could start the hard work of moving beyond what I had *been* and learning what I could *become*. I'd moved through denial, anger, *and* bargaining, some of them more than once. But that overwhelming weight of what I had lost, and the pain of everything I had experienced caused a wave of depression that felt more like an ocean.

In 2009 my moving trailer was stolen with everything I owned inside it. For literally *years* afterward I would reach for some sweater or a pair of earrings that I loved, only to remember they'd been in the trailer and I'd never see them again. The wave of depression beat me down just a little. But when I remembered that the quilt my recently deceased grandmother had lovingly made for me was *also* in that trailer, I would struggle for air. The depression hit all over again, almost every time I remembered these simple things. Some time later when I extracted myself from being trafficked, the depression was much deeper than anything I could've ever imagined. I'd lost more than an irreplaceable quilt. A large portion of who I had been no longer existed and I didn't know how to manage that. The depression sometimes caused me to launch backward, all the way back to anger and then belly flop back into the ocean of depression once more. My mental state bounced back and forth repeatedly as my former trafficker found new ways to try to attack me through the internet. I needed to get a handle on things. Finally I let the depression take over, as much as I didn't want to.

Often depression is misrepresented and people don't know exactly what it looks like. Would you know how to spot it in someone else?

Q: What do *you* think depression looks like in a friend or family member?

Q: How do you think people would spot depression in you?

Depression can show up in a lot of different ways. Are any of the following in your description from the above exercise?

- *Sadness*

- *Hopelessness*

- *Emptiness*

- *Sleeping too much or–*

- *Not being able to sleep enough*

- *Lack of energy*

- Avoiding things you enjoy, like hobbies
- Anxiety
- Restlessness
- Feelings of guilt, blame, shame,
- Feelings of worthlessness
- Increased food cravings or-
- Reduced appetite
- Brain fog
- Slower thinking process
- Reduced reaction time
- Memory issues
- Difficulty making decisions
- Irritability, anger, frustration
- Reduced sex drive
- Withdrawal from friendships

- *Thoughts of self-harm, death, or suicide*

I'm betting that since you're here, you probably did a pretty good job of outlining what forms of depression you've experienced personally. There are different degrees of depression, and many of the symptoms can overlap other health concerns, (such as thyroid disease in my case) so if you experience these symptoms for too long, please make sure you seek professional medical help.

Depression can have some pretty nasty and fairly serious impacts on your ability to perform everyday chores. If depression remains untreated (in serious cases) it can even put your life at risk But admitting that you are struggling with depression *does not automatically mean you are suicidal.* If you feel that you are struggling with suicidal thoughts, it's urgent that you seek assistance *immediately.* Because of the seriousness of depression and its symptoms, it's important to reach out for a medical or psychiatric professional to help you. There are several different treatment options available. If you do decide to speak to a medical professional about taking medication to help with your symptoms of depression there are many different things they might focus on.

You don't have to take the first medication or advice offered to you if you're not comfortable with it. Same goes when it comes to a therapist - we don't automatically get along with everyone we meet. It's not going to hurt a therapist's feelings if you don't think they're the right person for you. You can find someone who best suits your personality without feeling like you'll offend the therapist, too.

Some of the medications used to treat depression are selective serotonin reuptake inhibitors (SSNI), of which there are several on the market. Another option is the serotonin and noradrenaline reuptake inhibitors (SNRI), or tricyclic antidepressants (TCA). There are also monoamine oxidase inhibitors (MAOI), norepinephrine and dopamine reuptake inhibitors (NDRI), and more. If you prefer to take no medication at all, tell that to the doctors and they'll take it under advisement for treatment.

The idea of taking medications for depression can be really scary. It seems to solidify the facts even more, and that can be absolutely terrifying. But not having treatment when it can be incredibly helpful and beneficial is even worse.

Can you think of any other depression symptoms now that you've completed this chapter?

Chapter 8
Stage 5:
Acceptance

Okay, it happened. Now what?

It was 2018 and I was sitting in the *front row* of an anti-trafficking conference in Denver, Colorado. I'd been surviving from paycheck to paycheck and I couldn't afford the ticket to attend the event, but I desperately wanted to go, so a dear friend of mine bought the ticket and sent me to the event that would change my life forever. *(thank you, Bill K.)* As I listened to the panel of speakers on the stage, my mind reeled. I'd been suffering in silence for so many years, facing endless depression and anger spirals, believing it was all my life would ever be, and wondering why I should even choose to keep going. When they opened up the floor to questions, I raised my timid, withdrawn hand into the air, and the person with the microphone approached. My question I'd rehearsed in my head was to ask how long it took a survivor to find a functioning, healthy, normal life after surviving something so traumatic. What came out of my mouth instead left everyone in the room without words - including me.

"I - uh - I'm a survivor," I said into the mic, not even looking for any kind of sympathy, but rather for acknowledgment, *mainly from myself.* It was the first time I'd ever said the words, and I knew it wouldn't be the last, but that was **my** moment of acceptance. Eventually, after a long and awkward silence with 3,000 people in attendance, I followed it up with the question I'd originally intended to ask. I know most people are curious to know; the answer was exactly this:

It looks different for every survivor of any trauma.

Acceptance is that moment when you're finally in a position to move forward with your healing. At this point you've reached a place where you have processed and acknowledged what happened to you and you're in a better mindset to deal with the emotions and consequences of having gone through something so traumatic.

Many people believe that "acceptance" means forgiving the person who hurt you or even accepting what happened to you as being okay, but that's not the case at all. What it actually means is that you've come to terms with the fact that it happened at all and you understand that it's changed your life. It has nothing to do with forgiveness. In my case, and in the case of so many other trauma survivors, that comes quite some time later on down the road. Acceptance doesn't mean you don't get angry or depressed about it anymore, either. It's still entirely possible to bounce through the emotions still, and quite a common occurrence for so many. You can experience moments of sadness, grief, anger, and more. But when you reach this point, these emotions are more manageable. You're in a better place to deal with them finally.

It is INCREDIBLY IMPORTANT to not put too much pressure on yourself to get to this point. Healing is not a linear process and our brains move at their own pace. Trying to force yourself into the acceptance stage too soon can mean that you've not dealt with the other stages yet and they will eventually start to rear their ugly heads in your direction. Reaching the acceptance stage of your trauma journey can take a long time, sometimes many years as it took in my own case. You can move in and out of acceptance as you learn to accept some parts of the trauma and not yet others.

To help yourself through the acceptance stage, reach out for help when you need it. That help can come in the forms of friends and family, or mental health professionals. But you've done a lot of very hard work to reach this point of recovery and you should be proud of what you've accomplished.

Take the time to remind yourself of everything you've managed to accomplish since your trauma happened - from little victories to big ones. If you managed to make the bed on Tuesday, that counts. If you got a new job or moved to a new city, those are big things!

If you relearned how to walk again, that counts too. Every victory is important, and should be celebrated.

Q: What have you accomplished since your trauma?

I sincerely hope you've amassed quite the list of amazing things you've managed to accomplish in your journey through trauma survival so far, but if you haven't, there's still plenty of time. It's been a crazy journey for you, but you've made it this far.

Growth

from

Darkness

Book One – Stages of Trauma

Chapter 9
Starting the Discussion

Where do we begin?

Do you remember where you put that bookmark? If not, it was on the last page of chapter five, talking about anger. Take a moment to look at that list and think for a moment about how strong your feelings of anger were when you first experienced that overwhelming sensation, and compare them to how overwhelming it might feel now. While the anger is still very real and likely still very painful, it's not going to have that same white-hot rage of invisible fireworks popping behind your eyelids anymore. It's almost refreshing to know that the anger has eased up, isn't it?

If you ever took a tumble as a child and skinned your knee, it's likely you have a scar from that incident. I have several of my own - I was a pretty rough kid. Emotional trauma is no different than physical trauma in that aspect. When you've been injured, there are scars left behind that will likely be with you for the rest of your life. That doesn't mean a long ago scrape to your knee should prevent you from getting a good job or having a successful marriage, yet that's entirely too common among emotional trauma survivors who struggle with finding ways to move past what happened. Sometimes, the emotional scars cut much deeper than the physical scars.

In the first chapter I talked about how I've now found more productive ways to express who I am and what I've survived, rather than telling my experiences in a way that might cause some traumatic responses from other people. In the next "Growth from Darkness" book I'll be talking about trauma responses, and how we can each address them, but it's important to remember for now that sharing your deepest trauma with another trauma survivor can do more damage than you might be aware of. That doesn't mean you can't talk about what happened to you. You absolutely can! In fact, I make a living at it. It also doesn't mean that you *have to* talk about your trauma. But if you decide to, you can do it in a productive way that doesn't leave a wake of destruction behind you.

There are some healthy boundaries that are very important to recognize. When you take these things into consideration, it's easier to filter out what should and shouldn't be said in the company of friends or strangers.

Of course when you start talking about your trauma, it can be incredibly difficult and the emotions overwhelming. You might tear up. You might cry. You might, like I did, sob to the point of uncontrollable shaking. It does get easier as you go, if you choose to do it. But talking about your trauma with someone important in your life can be a huge help to you *and to them* when moving forward with your friendship or romantic relationship. If they don't know what your triggers might be, they don't know how to avoid them either. If they learn what your triggers are and then exploit them, that person shouldn't have the ability to reach you in any way from that point onward. That includes family members. Purposefully pushing the buttons of a trauma survivor is a form of exploitation and abuse.

The first step to learning how to talk about your trauma is to identify exactly why it is that you might be afraid to open up to someone. There are many reasons that people have cited, but there are many more beyond just these, also.

- *Fear of invalidation*
- *Fear of judgment*
- *Fear of victim blaming*
- *Fear of not being believed*
- *Fear of retribution or retaliation*
- *Fear of reliving the experience through memory*

Q: What other fears would you add to this list that might prevent you from speaking up about your trauma?

These are completely real concerns, and perfectly natural to experience. I've been through all of them myself. When I wrote "Custom Justice" I knew that I would need to relive all of the horrible details. The first time I spoke at a conference, I was terrified nobody would believe me - but they did. There are more people willing to listen than those who are not.

Some of the best tips I can provide for talking about your trauma would be as follows:

Find a supportive person.

This could be a close friend or trusted family member. Start with making a list of the most supportive people in your life, specifically those you feel like you've been able to talk to about anything that came up before the trauma. What are the pros and cons of telling each of these people? Are they going to get angry and react? Or will they listen to you when you tell them?

It's also important to consider the appropriateness of who it is you choose to speak with. If you're under the age of 18, talking to a trusted adult is one of the most important things you can do. If you don't trust your parents, try a teacher at school. If your trouble is specifically with a teacher, seek out a counselor, a parent, or even a grandparent. I know as a child I wasn't comfortable talking to my parents about a great many things because that fear of victim blaming had been validated too many times by one of my immediate family members. As an adult I didn't have many people I could talk to either, but I found an anti-trafficking organization that helped me to receive counseling when I needed it, at little to no cost for me. There are options available, but sometimes finding them can be a real challenge.

Grab out your notebook again and create a repeating list with three columns: People, Pros, Cons. Then begin listing the people you might consider talking to about your traumatic experience.

Once you've written down a list of people, write down all the reasons you can think of to talk to them, and all the reasons why talking to them might be a bad idea. Most of your listed people should have items in both columns. Take into consideration if these people have experienced their own similar traumas. Talking to them about yours might be extremely helpful because they had to learn how to get through it already, too. However, if they're not completely healed from their own trauma, speaking to them about it in detail might trigger some negative emotions within them, too. Try to be considerate to your safe person options.

Watch also for book 4 in the series, "Supporting Survivors" as this companion book might be very helpful to provide your safe person with.

Have compassion for yourself.

Unfortunately it's often the case that people who have survived trauma are rather unkind to themselves when bad things happen. There are many different reasons this happens, and it's a hard habit to break.

Make sure you provide yourself with what you need to find that kindness within, and to discover the grace you need to get through it. It takes an awful lot of courage and strength to talk about trauma with anyone, even a loved one. Make sure you talk to yourself like you would talk to someone you love. If it helps you to relax, light some candles, take some quiet time to yourself, and think of a few things to be grateful about.

Q: What are you grateful for at this moment?

Do you enjoy reading? Do you ever journal about your day? Do you have a favorite scented candle? What about a family pet who comforts and calms you? Maybe you have a favorite book to read.

Q: What are some of the nice things you've said to someone else that you think might apply to you, also?

Try to focus on things that are not related to physical appearance. Are you a good listener? Are you good at art or math? Do you show kindness to other people?

Sometimes it's really hard to think of nice things about ourselves, because we usually are our own worst critic. But if you came from the same kind of background I did, there have been enough bad things said *about* you and *to* you. It's time to change the way those people made us think about ourselves. It might not be an easy thing to do, but I promise it's worth it.

Confront Your Avoidance.

While it is really difficult to talk about your trauma, it's also sometimes very necessary for the healing process. That doesn't mean you have to talk about every little detail of what happened, but you can certainly discuss the effect it's had on your life and who you are going forward. It's extremely important to feel and express the natural emotions that will inevitably come up after experiencing your trauma, including sadness, fear, and the other stages of trauma already covered. Avoiding these things might have the extremely short term benefit of avoiding the uncomfortableness of it all, but it will *absolutely* and inevitably magnify your feelings of helplessness, powerlessness, and many other symptoms related to PTSD in the long term.

Short term solutions do long term damage.

When someone talks about a painful experience they've been through while in the company of a supportive, safe companion, our brains start to process the idea that trauma *can* be managed and those difficult, painful emotions are survivable. Your memories can be organized in a healthy way, rather than perpetuating the idea of self-blame and other fears listed again below. These very real fears start to slide to the recesses of our mind, and the healthy habits start to take precedence (more on this in book two).

- *Fear of invalidation*
- *Fear of judgment*
- *Fear of victim blaming*
- *Fear of not being believed*
- *Fear of retribution*
- *Fear of reliving the experience through memory*

Have you thought of other things that might hold you back from speaking to someone about your trauma? Have you thought of other people you might speak to about it?

Q: What else might hold you back from talking about what happened?

Tell Them What You Need

Whomever you've chosen to speak with about your traumatic experience and current mindset, make sure you tell that person *exactly* what you might need, if you know what that might be. You may need to discover some of it over time, but there are a few things that would likely come up right away. You might ask that person to make sure that in the future, they don't try to sneak up behind you to frighten you. One of the trauma symptoms is hypervigilance, and having someone sneak around with the purpose of frightening a trauma survivor can have some dramatic and unexpected results. It might be something as simple as asking the person not to touch your shoulders or reach out for a hug unexpectedly. You may even ask them not to respond to what you're about to tell them until you've finished speaking. Interruptions can be extremely distracting and can cause a person to retreat back into the mental shell of protection, feeling like they don't have the attention of the person they're with and don't feel safe telling them.

To make sure that you approach this subject with a healthy mindset, take the time to write out a do and don't list that you can look back on. Use this list to communicate with your person before AND after speaking with them about your trauma experience. Create four columns in your notebook. Name them as follows:

- Do (what I need now)
- Do not (what I don't need now)
- Future Do's (what I need from now on)
- Future Don'ts (please avoid from now on)

Some examples to list under each one:
For what to **do** now, you might ask someone to "listen" to you as you talk. You might ask them "**do not** interrupt" while you're telling them. For future ideas of what to do and what to avoid, think about what you're going to need. Will you need them to be patient while you learn to heal? Will you need them to avoid using hurtful phrases like telling you to get over it? This is a great place to start practicing some immediate healthy boundaries (more on this in book 3, Healthy Boundaries).

Writer a Letter

This one might be really hard for some people to understand, but it can be so much easier to write down what you want to communicate to someone, especially when speaking about difficult subjects. This was how I started my writing career - writing letters to people I didn't know how to talk to. When you sit down to talk to the person you want to talk too about your trauma, you can read your letter to them, or even use it as a guide to make sure you bring up certain bullet points that you fear you might forget to mention in a heightened emotional state. If you decide *not* to read the letter to them, you could use it just as a sort of 'rough draft' so you can decide on what you want to say and what you'd rather avoid talking about. There's another option for these letters too - something you'll learn in the next chapter.

Chapter 10
Taking Notes

You're on your way to a better life.

The average psychiatrist these days has no real training in the world of trauma or brain development. There are *some* trauma informed therapists and psychiatrists, but they can be hard to find. When a patient goes to see them and they have a problem, it's a knee-jerk reaction to diagnose them with a brain disease. Their first instinct is to give you some form of medication to help treat that brain imbalance. If you're depressed, the average psychiatrist might treat you with something to increase serotonin levels. Not many people are aware of this, but there is **absolutely no proof** that serotonin therapy helps the brain or symptoms of depression. That doesn't mean it can't help, because it might.

If you went to a friend's birthday while you were suffering with social anxiety, what would happen if you had a few beers? You might find that you're suddenly more sociable and friendly. It's possible that people wouldn't even know you ever had social anxiety in the first place. But does that mean your social anxiety is caused by the lack of alcohol in your bloodstream? Psychologists prescribe medications far too quickly for the symptoms of trauma and depression. That treatment is far too frequent, and usually for way too long. I heard a psychiatrist talking one day and discovered through him that somewhere in the neighborhood of 25% of women in the USA are on some kind of psychiatric medication. Considering that around 60% of men and 50% of women experience a traumatic event in their lifetime and most don't report it, the percentage of people on psychiatric medication doesn't seem to be that much of a coincidence.

When a person becomes stable on psychiatric medications, that *should* be the moment that the real treatment starts. Unfortunately it's not. Too often, that's when the treatment ends, and the suffering person is left with only medication for help. People should be able to deal with their traumas and emotions, but when psychiatric medications are prescribed so freely, that ability is taken away. Learning to talk about our trauma, and how to process what we've been through, are the first steps to moving beyond just having medication shoved at us, and learning how to manage what's going on inside.

Talking about trauma is not an easy thing, but I'm hopeful that you've found a few good places to start with that might guide you in the right direction. There are many resources online for you to research on your own if you need additional help with any of these chapters, or you can always write directly to Growth from Darkness. You can join the Facebook group and talk with other alumni going through the series, or you can send an email directly to the GFD team.

www.facebook.com/groups/growthfromdarkness
GrowthFromDarkness@gmail.com

I wish you all the best of luck on your healing journey, and when you're ready to start tackling those PTSD and trauma responses, just look for Growth from Darkness, book two. I'll be ready for you.

If you've found yourself getting emotional benefit from writing down what you're thinking, feeling, or struggling with, please continue to write! It's been such a great help in my own journey and I know the benefits to it so well. I'd like to encourage you *again* to join the Growth from Darkness group on Facebook so you can talk to others who have been or are going through the same things.

Another trick I learned in my therapy classes was to write letters to people who wronged me in some way - letters I have no intention of ever sending - and then therapeutically burning the letter in a controlled environment to mitigate the danger of a fire spreading. I've burned letters to my mother in a church fire pit, letters to my former trafficker in a wood burning fireplace, and letters to myself at a campfire.

Q: If you were to write a letter you intended to burn, who would it be to?

Nobody should ever force you to tell your story of what happened, but sometimes just telling it to yourself can be the best therapy we could ever ask for.

Growth

From

Darkness

will continue with book two,

Trauma Reactions

Growth

from

Darkness

Book One – Stages of Trauma

About the Author

Amanda Blackwood is an accomplished artist and author, public speaker, podcast host, trauma recovery mentor and a survivor of human trafficking. Amanda lives in Denver, Colorado with her rescue cats and supportive husband who keep her sane. Find more books by Amanda Blackwood at your favorite online book retailer.

A portion of all proceeds from every book sold will go to local organizations that help fight human trafficking here in the USA. Please consider leaving a review online if you've enjoyed this book. We hope you leave a kind word that will encourage others to pick up this book written from the heart with the intention of helping others heal from a traumatic past.

www.ingramcontent.com/pod-product-compliance
Lightning Source LLC
Chambersburg PA
CBHW052219150726
48002CB00003B/1177